· PEOPLES of NORTH AMERICA ·

Inuit

VALERIE BODDEN

CREATIVE EDUCATION · CREATIVE PAPERBACKS

Published by Creative Education and Creative Paperbacks
P.O. Box 227, Mankato, Minnesota 56002
Creative Education and Creative Paperbacks
are imprints of The Creative Company
www.thecreativecompany.us

Design and production by Christine Vanderbeek
Art direction by Rita Marshall
Printed in China

Photographs by Alamy (Alan King Etching 07, ClassicStock, Design Pics Inc, Robert Huberman, imageBROKER, ton koene, Paul Andrew Lawrence, Nature Picture Library, The Print Collector, Science History Images), Creative Commons Wikimedia (After Hieronimo Custodis; Edward S. Curtis; George R. King/National Geographic Magazine; Lomen Bros., Nome/Library of Congress; Unknown; Zentralbibliothek Zürich), Getty Images (Doug Allan, Bettmann, Margaret Bourke-White/ The LIFE Picture Collection, De Agostini/M. Seemuller, Mario De Biasi/ Mondadori Portfolio, Remsberg Inc, White Fox/AGF/UIG), iStockphoto (duncan1890, Adrian Wojcik), Pixabay (skeeze), Shutterstock (Alexandr Junek Imaging, Bildagentur Zoonar GmbH, Mike Clime, SMIRNOVA IRINA, JNB Photography, OHishiapply, Transia Design), Smithsonian Institution (Department of Anthropology, Smithsonian Institution/National Museum of the American Indian)

Library of Congress Cataloging-in-Publication Data
Names: Bodden, Valerie, author.
Title: Inuit / Valerie Bodden.
Series: Peoples of North America.
Includes bibliographical references and index.
Summary: A history of the people and events that influenced the North American Indian tribe known as the Inuit, including the Inuit Circumpolar Council and conflicts such as early encounters with Europeans on Baffin Island.
Identifiers: LCCN 2017044009 / ISBN 978-1-60818-966-3 (hardcover)
ISBN 978-1-62832-593-5 (pbk) / ISBN 978-1-64000-067-4 (eBook)
Subjects: LCSH: 1. Inuit—Juvenile literature. 2. Inuit—History—Juvenile literature.
Classification: LCC E99.E7 B6745 2018 / DDC 971.9004/9712—dc23

CCSS: RI.5.1, 2, 3, 5, 6, 8, 9; RH.6-8.4, 5, 6, 7, 8, 9

First Edition HC 9 8 7 6 5 4 3 2 1
First Edition PBK 9 8 7 6 5 4 3 2 1

PEOPLES of NORTH AMERICA

Inuit

VALERIE BODDEN

CREATIVE EDUCATION • CREATIVE PAPERBACKS

Table of Contents

AN INUIT WOMAN IN THE EARLY 1900S (ON PAGE 3);
A POLAR BEAR SKIN STRETCHED OUT IN A DRYING
FRAME IN GREENLAND (PICTURED HERE).

· INUIT ·

Introduction

PEOPLES of NORTH AMERICA

For hundreds of years, the Inuit people have made their home in the **ARCTIC**. This region presented some of the harshest conditions on the planet. During the long winters, temperatures could drop to -80 °F (-62.2 °C). Fierce winds howled across the snow. For several months out of the year, the sun remained hidden below the horizon, leaving the frozen world in perpetual darkness. But the Arctic was not barren. During the brief summer months of 24-hour sunlight, the **TUNDRA** bloomed with low-growing flowers, grasses, and lichens. Caribou, muskoxen, and wolves roamed the land, while seals, whales, and walruses swam the cold ocean waters. The region's clear rivers teemed with fish, and great flocks of migratory birds landed on the tundra. For the Inuit, life revolved around these animals, which they relied on for food, clothing, and shelter.

The name "Inuit" means "the people." (A single Inuit person is referred to as an Inuk.) In the past, the Inuit were called Eskimos. This was once thought to mean "eaters of raw fish." Now it is thought to mean "snowshoe netters." Today, the **INDIGENOUS** people of Greenland and Canada prefer the term Inuit. In Alaska, many native peoples still use the word Eskimo, which can refer to both the Inuit and the related **YUPIK** peoples. For centuries, the Inuit remained isolated in the Arctic. But when their way of life was threatened by European and American influences, the Inuit adapted. They accepted some of the new ways while also fighting to hold on to their traditional culture.

ALASKA'S DENALI NATIONAL PARK IS HOME
TO THE TALLEST PEAK IN NORTH AMERICA.

The Inuit call the earliest Arctic peoples *Tuniit*, or "the first peoples." Many **ANTHROPOLOGISTS** believe the Tuniit reached North America by boat from **SIBERIA** around 3000 B.C. Over time, they spread eastward across much of northern Alaska and northern Canada and into Greenland. Around A.D. 1200, the Tuniit encountered newcomers: the Inuit. Although the Inuit had initially remained along the Alaskan coast, they now pushed across the continent. Interactions between the Tuniit and Inuit may have led to conflict in some cases. In others, the two cultures may have melded through intermarriage. Soon, the Inuit culture had largely replaced that of the Tuniit.

Although related by language and culture, the Inuit did not consider themselves a single tribe. Anthropologists who study the Inuit divide them into three cultural groups, based on location: the Alaska Inuit (which includes the Inuit of Siberia), the Central Inuit of Canada, and the Greenland Inuit. Each group can be further divided into numerous smaller groups, or bands, based on geography, **DIALECT**, and culture. The various bands were spread 3,200 miles (5,150 km) across Siberia, Alaska, Canada, and Greenland, and each spoke its own dialect of the Inuktitut language. However, the dialects

ARCTIC PEOPLES HAVE BEEN SUSTAINABLY HUNT-
ING SEALS FOR THE ANIMALS' SKIN AND MEAT FOR
HUNDREDS OF YEARS.

SOME GREENLAND
INUIT TENTS WERE
MADE ENTIRELY
OF CARIBOU SKINS,
AND LARGE STONES
SECURED THEIR
BASES.

remained similar enough that an Inuk could communicate with people from most other Inuit bands, no matter where they lived.

Most Inuit bands lived near the coasts of the Pacific, Atlantic, or Arctic oceans, although some lived inland. Some Inuit bands set up permanent or semi-permanent villages. A village might have as few as 10 to 50 people, or it might have a population in excess of 800. Many Inuit spent the winter in villages but then split up into single families to live as **NOMADIC** hunters.

For summer hunts, families often lived in cone- or dome-shaped tents. The tent frames were constructed of driftwood or whalebone. They were covered with sealskin or caribou hide. But the Arctic winter called for more substantial shelter. Throughout most of the Arctic, the Inuit lived in *karmats*. These semi-subterranean homes had rectangular walls made of stones or logs and were covered with thick sod. People entered the karmat through a long underground tunnel to keep out the cold. An animal-skin flap served as a door. Inside, the karmat had 1 to 3 rooms, each about 10 square feet (0.9 sq m). Stretched animal intestines served as windows or skylights. Coastal Inuit heated their homes with the fat from sea mammals, called blubber. A home heated with blubber could reach 90 °F (32 °C), even in the heart of winter.

In some villages, the Inuit also built larger structures known as *karigi* or *kashims*. These buildings were used for ceremonies, dances, sweat baths, and storytelling. In some communities, they also served as sleeping quarters for the men of the village.

Although people today tend to associate the Inuit with igloos, only the Inuit of northern Canada built igloos. These were used as temporary shelters while moving or hunting in the winter. It took an Inuit man about an hour to build an igloo. First, he used a long

BENEFITS OF RAW MEAT *With few fruit or vegetable resources, the Inuit had to rely on meat for nearly all their nutritional needs. Scientists have found that by eating meat raw, the Inuit were able to take in large amounts of vitamins stored in the animals' tissues. For example, whale skin was a good source of vitamin C, while raw liver provided vitamins A and D. In addition, the fat from these animals provided the Inuit with an important source of energy.*

DESPITE THE POLAR BEAR'S ENDANGERED STATUS, CANADIAN INUIT ARE ALLOWED TO HUNT A LIMITED NUMBER EACH YEAR.

knife of bone or ivory to cut large blocks of hard-packed snow. The builder then arranged the blocks in a circle about 10 to 15 feet (3–4.6 m) in diameter. He trimmed the tops of the blocks to slope inward. Then he stacked a new layer of blocks on top of the first. He kept stacking snow blocks until he had created a perfect dome shape, about 10 to 12 feet (3–3.7 m) high. A small hole was left at the top to allow smoke to escape. Sometimes, clear ice or animal intestines were used to create windows. A layer of snow was packed around the outside of the igloo to provide insulation. Inside, a blubber lamp was used to melt the interior walls. The walls were then allowed to quickly refreeze into a smooth glaze of ice that blocked the wind. Low benches and sleeping platforms made with hard-packed snow were covered with twigs and furs to provide warmth.

To move from place to place in the Arctic, the Inuit relied on boats and sleds. They built two kinds of boats. The one- or two-person kayak had a frame of driftwood or whalebone. Stretched skins from seals or other animals covered the frame. The larger umiak was also made of driftwood or whalebone covered with sealskin, but it had a flat bottom for greater stability. At 15 to 50 feet (4.6–15.2 m) long and 5 feet (1.5 m) wide, an umiak could hold

POLAR BEAR HUNT *Prized for both their meat and their fur, nanuq, or polar bears, were pursued by only the bravest hunters. They were usually hunted on sea ice in the dark of winter. Often, hunters sent their dogs to charge the bear first. With the bear cornered, the hunter moved in close enough to kill it with a* HARPOON *or spear. Afterward, the hunter ate a piece of the polar bear's meat to show his respect for the animal.*

10 or more people.

On land, travel required the use of sleds pulled by people or dogs. Sleds consisted of a platform made of wood or animal skins attached to runners of wood or bone. The runners were covered with water that froze to form a sleek surface that would slip across the ice and snow.

Because few edible plants grew in the Arctic, the Inuit ate mostly meat. "We Inupiat are meat eaters, not vegetarians," said Alaskan Inuk Jonah Tokienna. "We live off the sea mammals.... The Bering Sea and the Chukchi Sea are our gardens." Sea mammals—especially seals—were important to almost all coastal Inuit bands. Some Inuit also took whales and walruses. Among land animals, caribou were inland Inuit's most important food source. Freshwater fish also made up a significant portion of some bands' diets. The Inuit often ate meat raw, although they also boiled it or dipped it in sauces. Food to be stored for the winter was sun-dried or frozen. The Inuit used every part of the animals they hunted. Blubber was burned for light and heat; skins could be used to make clothing, blankets, and boat covers; **SINEW** served as thread; and bones and teeth were fashioned into a variety of tools.

WRAPPED IN WARM
CARIBOU FURS
(ABOVE), INUIT
CRAFTSMEN USED
BOW DRILLS TO
MAKE IVORY TOOLS
(RIGHT) OR START
FIRES.

In addition to using these goods themselves, the Inuit traded with their neighbors. Each year, thousands of Inuit gathered for trade fairs. Inuit bands from the coast offered blubber, sealskins, and ivory to inland bands in exchange for caribou skins, other furs, and snowshoes. The Inuit also traded with American Indian and **FIRST NATIONS** peoples.

War does not seem to have been common among the Inuit, but at times feuds between neighboring Inuit villages did occur. If an Inuk from one family killed an Inuk from another family, it could lead to a feud that lasted generations. The Inuit also had enemies among nearby American Indian and First Nations peoples, including the Cree and the Chipewyan.

As they went about their yearly cycle of trading, hunting, and traveling, the Inuit were always aware of their close ties to the land. Despite its myriad threats, this was the land that supplied the people with everything they needed. They couldn't imagine a time when it wouldn't be theirs alone.

I nuit life centered on the extended family—including parents, children and their families, and grandparents—rather than on the band. Even in villages, the Inuit did not recognize a chief or official leader, although older men who had shown strong hunting skills might be consulted for informal guidance. Within the family, the oldest man still able to hunt generally held the role of leader. Sometimes, two or more related families shared a home and traveled and hunted together. This increased the chances of survival for each. Generosity was greatly valued among the Inuit. Meat was freely given to those in need. A home abandoned by a family that had left to hunt was considered free for anyone's use. As author David Pelly explains, "According to ancient Inuit philosophy, sharing among all beings makes survival in the Arctic possible. A real Inuk would never … decline to share the hunt's reward, for to do so would be to contravene [go against] the basic laws of respect among all creatures."

Hunting was the most important aspect of survival in the Arctic. Huge numbers of animals needed to be killed to satisfy an adult's dietary need for meat—up to eight pounds (3.6 kg) a day. The animals available varied by season and location.

SOME EARLY EUROPEAN EXPLORERS STUDIED THE INUIT LIFESTYLE AND ADOPTED THEIR TECHNIQUES TO SURVIVE THE HARSH SURROUNDINGS.

During the summer months, Inuit men used kayaks to hunt seals in open water.

In the winter, when a layer of ice six feet (1.8 m) thick or more coated the ocean, many coastal Inuit hunted seals. With the help of his dogs, a hunter located an *allu*, or seal's breathing hole, in the ice. He waited over the hole, sometimes for hours. As the seal came up, the hunter speared it with his harpoon. Afterward, he widened the hole in the ice to pull the seal through.

In the spring, hunters crawled on their bellies to sneak up on seals sunning themselves on the ice. Other men hunted seals from kayaks.

Among some Inuit bands, whales provided an even more vital food source than seals. An *umialik*, or umiak captain, headed a crew of six to eight whale hunters. As the ice broke up in the spring, the umialik and his crew pulled their boat to the edge of the ice, watching for a whale to spout. When they spotted one, they quickly paddled out to it. A man designated as the harpooner drove a harpoon into the whale's head or a spot behind the pectoral fin. Floats made of inflated sealskins were attached to the harpoon. As the whale tried to swim away, these floats dragged at it, quickly tiring the animal. Once exhausted, the whale surfaced, and the men speared it.

In the summer, sea-based hunting turned to the migratory walrus and sea lion that came north for the warmer months. The walrus was one of the Inuit's most dangerous prey animals. A male walrus weighs up to 3,700 pounds (1,678 kg). With its sharp tusks, it isn't afraid to charge human hunters. But walrus skin was highly desired for kayak and umiak coverings, and the ivory from the animals' long tusks could be carved into both useful tools

PARTNERS *Although an Inuk man's closest ties were to family, he sometimes established formal partnerships with an unrelated Inuk. The bonds between partners were considered as strong as the bonds between family members. For example, men who were "sharing partners" shared food with one another's families. "Song partners" performed religious rituals together. They might also temporarily share wives. Men or women who shared a name became "name partners" and gave each other gifts.*

and beautiful items.

On land, caribou was highly desired prey. Some inland bands hunted caribou year-round. Coastal bands often moved inland for the summer to hunt caribou as well. Hunters working alone might creep up on a caribou and spear it or shoot it with a bow and arrow. At other times, bands participated in group hunts. First, they set up a long, V-shaped path bordered by large piles of rocks or sod. Women and children hid nearby. When a caribou herd approached, they waved their arms to frighten the animals. They chased the caribou along the path, which led into a lake or a large corral. There the men could easily spear or shoot the animals.

Summer was also a prime time for river fishing. The Inuit took trout, Arctic char, and whitefish with hooks, nets, **WEIRS**, and spears. They sometimes built dams to trap **SPAWNING** salmon.

While men spent most of their time hunting and fishing, women prepared food, melted ice to obtain drinking water, and made clothing. Most Inuit clothing was made from caribou skin, although the hides of polar bears, wolves, foxes, and squirrels were also used. Men and women wore the same type of clothing, which included a parka, pants, boots, and mittens. The parka, or jacket, had two layers. The inside layer had the fur facing inward, while the outside layer had the fur facing out. A woman's parka also had a large *amaut*, or hood, for carrying babies. For rainy weather or seafaring, women made water-resistant jackets from sealskin or seal intestines. Sealskin and caribou fur were also used to make *mukluks*, or boots.

In addition to making clothing, women cared for the children. Inuit babies were often named after a relative or friend who had recently died. The baby was believed to inherit that person's spirit. According to Inuk Armand Tagoona, "An Inuk believes that when you name your child after the dead one, then the dead

BASED ON 3,000-YEAR-OLD DNA EVIDENCE, SOME SCIENTISTS BELIEVE INUIT ANCESTORS CAME FROM EASTERN ASIA.

one lives again in the name, and the spirit of the dead one has a body again." Inuit children spent much of their time at play. But they were also taught survival skills at a young age. Both boys and girls learned to drive a sled, assess animal tracks, and interpret the weather. Between the ages of five and eight, young boys learned to use weapons. By 10 or 11, they began to hunt with their fathers. Meanwhile, around age seven, girls began to help their mothers cut ice for drinking water. By the time they were 10, they helped care for younger siblings.

For the Inuit, religion was part of everyday life. They believed that everything—from people to animals, plants, and inanimate objects—contained a spirit, or *inua*. Some Inuit bands also believed in a divine female called Sedna who watched over sea mammals. They sought to keep both the animals and Sedna happy so that the prey would continue to give themselves freely as food. Maintaining harmony with the inua required performing special rituals before and during a hunt. For example, sea mammals were

REINDEER HERDING *In the 1890s, as native Arctic animal populations declined, the United States government and Christian missionaries encouraged the Inuit to try reindeer herding. More than 1,000 reindeer were introduced from Siberia. But reindeer tending did not mesh well with the Inuit lifestyle. Reindeer need to move frequently to find new grazing grounds, which meant the Inuit couldn't spend time in their villages. When they wanted to go out hunting, they had to leave the herd. These issues led the Inuit to give up reindeer herding by the 1930s.*

given a drink of cold, fresh water after they were killed. Land animals were also given gifts, such as knives. Some Inuit also sewed sacred amulets, or charms, onto their clothing to gain the spirits' favor. The amulets might be small animals carved from ivory or the claws, teeth, or other parts of an animal.

In addition to hunting rituals, some Inuit bands observed ceremonies such as the Bladder Dance. During this ceremony, they inflated the bladders of sea mammals—which were thought to hold the animals' souls—with air. They then returned the bladders to the sea. For some ceremonies, men wore carved masks. Women wore tiny versions of the masks on their fingers. Ceremonies were often led by an *angakok*, or **SHAMAN**. The shaman also performed healing rituals, attempted to control the weather, and predicted the future.

RELATED TO WILD CARIBOU, DOMESTIC REINDEER WERE USED AS PACK ANIMALS FOR GOLD MINERS IN THE EARLY 1900S.

The Inuit of Greenland may have been the first native people in the Western Hemisphere to meet with Europeans. In A.D. 984, a group of Vikings led by **ERIK THE RED** landed in Greenland and established a settlement there. However, the Vikings and Inuit likely had little contact.

The next recorded meeting between Inuit and Europeans did not occur until 1576, when British explorer **MARTIN FROBISHER** landed on Canada's Baffin Island. Frobisher headed a crew searching for the Northwest Passage, a water route connecting the Atlantic and Pacific oceans. According to Inookie Adamie, "During the first meeting, the Inuit were just in awe. The *qallunaat* ["big eyebrows," the Inuit word for Europeans] came with their huge ship. The Inuit themselves had only sealskin boats…. They had never seen a ship. They had never heard a shot…. When they met there was a lot of uncertainty. The Inuit were scared. They didn't want to give in to these people because they didn't know what they were. Because they weren't quite Inuit. And their clothes—how they dressed!… They were different beings…. We knew their clothes would never protect them from the cold…. They were ghostly."

The meeting between Frobisher's crew and the Inuit began peacefully but soon deteriorated. After trading fish and sealskin clothing for European-made

BELIEVING HE HAD FOUND GOLD, MARTIN FROBISHER BROUGHT MORE THAN 1,200 TONS (1.089 T) OF FOOL'S GOLD, OR IRON PYRITE, BACK TO ENGLAND.

THE CAPTIVES
FROM FROBISHER'S
SECOND VOYAGE
INCLUDED AN
INUIT MOTHER
AND HER CHILD.

items, the Inuit took five English crewmen back to their camp. When they failed to return to the ship, Frobisher and his remaining crew fled, fearing the other men had been captured. As they left, they kidnapped an Inuit man. The man died shortly after the ship reached England.

The following summer, Frobisher returned to Baffin Island, bringing a larger crew with him. Although things again started well, a battle broke out after Frobisher attempted to force two Inuit to come with him to serve as interpreters. Although the Inuit wounded Frobisher, their stone-tipped arrows were no match for European firearms. Frobisher's crew killed many of the Inuit. Others jumped from cliffs into the sea to escape. But three captives were taken back to England. All three died shortly after arrival.

When Frobisher made a third expedition to Baffin Island, the Inuit remained hidden and refused to supply his crew. In response, Frobisher condemned them as "brutish and uncivil people." He returned to England without having found the Northwest Passage.

After Frobisher, explorers from England, France, Portugal, and Spain continued the quest to locate the Northwest Passage for the next 300 years. Some traded with the Inuit, providing them with metal knives, tools, and even guns in return for meat and

⇒ TO THE NORTH POLE ⇐ *In the early 1900s, explorers from around the world raced to become the first to reach the North Pole. Before making his attempt, American explorer Robert Peary lived among the Inuit of Greenland, studying their language, culture, and clothing. He learned to make igloos, dig CACHES, and drive a dogsled. In April 1909, Peary led an expedition to the North Pole. Among the expedition's crew were four Inuit men, who proved to be instrumental to the mission's success.*

fur clothing. At times, these encounters became violent. But some
Europeans maintained friendly relations with the Inuit, whom
they grew to admire. In 1821, for example, an expedition led by
British explorers William Edward Parry and George Francis Lyon
became icebound for two winters. Local Inuit taught the explorers
to build igloos and dogsleds. Afterward, Lyon reported, "I verily
believe that there does not exist a more honest set of people than
the tribe with whom we had so long an acquaintance."

Even as European explorers continued to arrive from the east,
Russian explorers approached North America from the west. In
July 1728, **VITUS BERING**, a Danish explorer serving as a captain in
the Russian navy, led an expedition through the strait that sepa-
rates eastern Asia from western North America. (The waterway
would later become known as the Bering Strait.) Although visibil-
ity on this first expedition was too poor to spot the North American
coastline, the trip sparked enough interest to mount additional
journeys. In 1741, Bering led a second expedition to North America.
This time, he made landfall in present-day Alaska. Unfortunately,
Bering's ship was eventually wrecked, and he and many of his
crew died during the harsh winter. Survivors returned to Russia,

⊸⊶ NANOOK OF THE NORTH ⊷⊸ *In 1922,* Nanook of the North: A Story of Life and Love in the Actual Arctic *was released as the first documentary film. Filmed in northern Quebec, the movie traces the daily activities of an Inuk man as he hunts, trades, and builds an igloo. The film's release sparked widespread interest in the Inuit (then called Eskimo) and even led to products such as Eskimo Pie ice cream bars. Recently, however, the film was shown to have been largely staged.*

where they spoke of the abundant populations of fur-bearing animals inhabiting North America.

Russian fur traders soon set out for Alaska. At first, they remained in the Aleutian Islands, where they came in contact with the **ALEUT** people. When voluntary trade did not provide enough sea otter furs, beaver pelts, and sealskins for the Russian market, the traders compelled the Aleut to meet fur quotas by taking their families hostage. The families of hunters who failed to meet their quotas were executed. As the Russians pushed eastward, they sometimes met with resistance, but their superior firepower often won out. By the early 1800s, Russian trading posts had been set up throughout southern Alaska. Contact with these trading posts brought the Inuit glass beads and metal objects.

The Inuit of Alaska had direct contact with Europeans when British explorer Captain **JAMES COOK** stopped briefly at Norton Sound in 1778. Meanwhile, Samuel Hearne, working on behalf of the Hudson's Bay Company, reached the Inuit of northern Canada. Hearne offered the Inuit steel traps, guns, sugar, and coffee in return for animal hides and furs. In Greenland, Scottish explorer John Ross encountered the Polar Inuit—the northernmost

WHALERS BROUGHT
FOREIGN GOODS,
BUT MANY INUIT
CONTINUED TO
HUNT IN ORDER
TO TRADE ANIMAL
SKINS (RIGHT).

population in the world—in 1818. He reported, "They exist in a corner of the world by far the most secluded which has yet been discovered, … until the moment of our arrival [they] believed themselves to be the only inhabitants of the universe, and that all the rest of the world was a mass of ice."

Although these encounters led to increasing contact with nonnative peoples, the Inuit were perhaps most affected by the arrival of hundreds of European and American whaling ships in the mid-1800s. The whalers wanted whale oil from blubber, to be used for making soaps and candles. They also needed baleen, the long, comblike structures in a whale's mouth used for straining food from the water. Baleen could be used to make corset stays, buttons, and even fishing rods. Some Inuit traded with the whalers, while others put their skills to work on commercial whaling ships. They were paid with flour, molasses, guns, and alcohol.

The availability of these trade goods led to changes in traditional Inuit culture. Durable metal pots replaced stone and hide ones. Steel knives were used in place of bone, and kerosene, rather than blubber, fueled lamps. Working for whalers, the Inuit had less time for hunting and other traditional activities. As a result, many became dependent upon trade goods for food and other necessities. The introduction of alcohol had a devastating impact. In addition, European diseases such as smallpox, influenza, and measles spread among the Inuit. Adding to the hardship, overhunting led to the depletion of many animal populations, including whale, seal, walrus, and caribou. This caused starvation among Inuit bands. From an estimated 60,000 before European contact, Inuit numbers dropped to 30,000 by 1900.

· INUIT ·

Mixing New and Old

PEOPLES of NORTH AMERICA

In 1867, the U.S. purchased the Alaska Territory from Russia. Afterward, the number of traders and whalers on Inuit lands increased. The discovery of gold near Nome, Alaska, in 1898 brought more than 40,000 prospectors. Some passed through or even stayed in Inuit communities. In other cases, Inuit moved closer to mining camps to find work.

In addition to traders and prospectors, missionaries arrived in Inuit territory. The Russian Orthodox Church had already established missions in many Aleut and Yupik communities during the heyday of the Russian fur trade. Now Protestant missionaries moved into Inuit communities in northern Alaska and Canada. In many villages, they set up boarding, or "residential," schools and medical services.

Public schools were established throughout Alaska and Canada in the 1940s and '50s. Often, these schools were located in large communities. Children from smaller communities had to travel far from home to attend. At school, they were not allowed to speak their own language or practice their traditional culture. Marius Tungilik, who attended such an institution, felt that the schools taught students "to hate our own people, basically, our own kind." He said that after attending school, "you begin to think and see your

IN THE REMOTE CANADIAN TERRITORY OF NUNA-
VUT, FORMAL PUBLIC SCHOOLS HAVE EXISTED ONLY
SINCE THE 1950S.

own people in a different light. You see them eating with their hands. You think, 'Okay, primitive.'" At many schools, students died as a result of illness, abuse, and neglect.

Despite continuing problems with schools, the 1950s brought improved healthcare overall. Inuit populations that had been decimated by disease began to rebound. Many communities began to adopt modern ways. By the 1960s, Inuit villages incorporated stores, churches, and even airstrips. Since the whaling and fur industries had dried up decades earlier, many Inuit worked wage-paying jobs in construction, fish canning, and other industries.

Even as they accepted many new ways, the Inuit began to push for greater recognition of their land rights. In 1971, the Alaska Native Claims Settlement Act (ANCSA) gave the Inuit and other Alaska natives ownership of 44 million acres (17.8 million ha)—about 12 percent of the total land area of Alaska. The settlement also provided $962.5 million to be used for economic development. In return, the Inuit agreed to allow the government to build the Trans-Alaska Pipeline through their territory.

Meanwhile, in Canada, some Inuit communities had faced forcible relocation in the 1950s. Proclaiming that the action would increase hunting opportunities for the Inuit, the government moved people more than 1,000 miles (1,609 km) north. Many who

⟶ **ESKIMO-INDIAN OLYMPICS** ⟶ *Since 1961, the annual World Eskimo-Indian Olympics have celebrated traditional games played by the Inuit. Among the most popular events are the one-foot and two-foot high kick events, in which an athlete has to kick an object suspended in the air. Athletes in the one-hand reach must stretch to touch a suspended target while balancing their body on one hand. In the nalukataq, or blanket toss, an athlete is tossed up to 30 feet (9.1 m) into the air from a seal or walrus skin.*

had previously lived below the Arctic Circle now lived within 900 miles (1,448 km) of the North Pole. For shelter, they were given only tents. "It was like landing on the moon," said John Amagoalik, who was six years old when his family was relocated. "There was absolutely nothing but gray gravel and snow." Anna Nungaq said that after being relocated, "I hardly slept for years, cried, wanting to go home.... I did not think there would ever be a day of light again.... Because I had never been in a place where there is no daylight at all, I was so scared and thought there would never be light again."

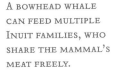

A BOWHEAD WHALE CAN FEED MULTIPLE INUIT FAMILIES, WHO SHARE THE MAMMAL'S MEAT FREELY.

The Canadian Inuit fight for land rights began in the 1960s. It was resolved in 1999, when the Canadian government created the territory of Nunavut. Inuktitut for "Our Land," Nunavut covers 800,000 square miles (2.1 million sq km) of northern Canada. About 85 percent of Nunavut's 37,000 people are Inuit. The Canadian government also gave the Inuit $1.14 billion. In 2010, it issued a formal apology for the Inuit relocations of the 1950s.

Today, a total of 155,000 Inuit live in Alaska, Canada, Greenland, and Russia. Despite being spread across countries, the Inuit work together through the Inuit Circumpolar Council (ICC), which was established in 1977. "While we are divided by four political boundaries, our common languages, traditions, and ancestry give us common bond and strength to work together," said Caleb Pungowiyi, former president of the ICC.

Among the issues the ICC has addressed are Inuit whaling and seal hunting rights. In 1986, the International Whaling Commission (IWC) issued a ban on whaling. The organization made an exception for Inuit hunters, however, who were given quotas they could not exceed. From 2013 to 2018, Alaskan Inuit were permitted to take a total of 306 bowhead whales, for example.

In 2009, the European Union placed a ban on imported seal

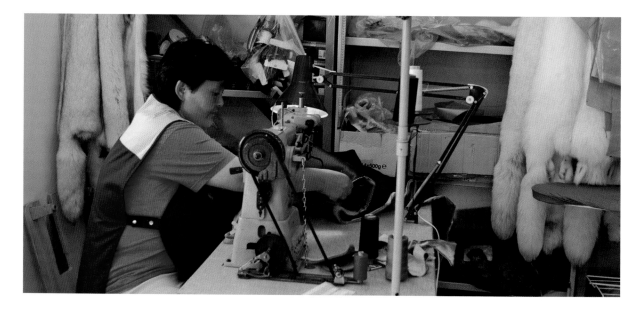

THE INUIT FACE
GROWING THREATS
TO THEIR SURVIVAL
AS SEA LEVELS RISE,
COASTS ERODE
(RIGHT), AND
INCOMES FALL.

products. Although the ban was not meant to apply to products made by traditional Inuit hunters and craftspeople, the market for seal products disappeared as a result. Many Inuit families were left with no way to make a living. Former ICC president Duane Smith said that those who supported the ban "don't see the people, the communities, or the way of life they are ruining." Mary Simon, the former president of a Canadian organization dedicated to Inuit well-being, agreed. She vowed that the "Inuit will continue to hunt seals, develop modern sealskin fashions, and create new markets for these products. We will not have our way of life dictated by European leaders who we believe are being duped by animal rights activists."

Another issue facing the Inuit in recent years has been climate change. "In the North, climate change is not something that may happen in the future; it's something that is happening now," said Sheila Watt-Cloutier, former chair of the ICC. "It's not just about polar bears; it is about people and a way of life." Many Inuit have noted that sea ice forms later and melts earlier than in the past. In some places, the ice is too thin, resulting in hunters falling through.

Today, life in Inuit communities has changed drastically. In Alaska, about half of all Inuit live in urban areas. Rather than

→ ⚜ **$68 WATERMELON** ⚜ ← *Many Inuit continue to eat traditional foods such as seal, caribou, and fish. But stores offer other foods as well. Getting these foods to remote villages is costly. This leads to high food prices. A gallon (3.8 L) of milk that costs $4.40 in Ottawa, Canada, for example, costs $12.99 in remote northern villages. A can of soup may sell for $11. Fresh fruits and vegetables are even more expensive. A head of cabbage might go for $28, and a watermelon for $68.*

traditional homes, many Inuit now live in wooden houses on stilts or gravel pads that provide insulation from the frozen ground underneath. For most Inuit, factory-made clothes have replaced traditional caribou-skin clothing. Rather than kayaks and dogsleds, many Inuit now travel by motorboats, snowmobiles, and other vehicles. In place of harpoons and bows and arrows, most hunters use guns. Not all Inuit hunt anymore, either. Those who do hunt may also take summer jobs.

Despite these changes, many Inuit continue to hold on to aspects of their traditional culture. Some schools offer classes in native languages and culture. Even those Inuit who live in cities can take trips north to relearn Inuit hunting and fishing practices. In some communities, traditional Inuit ceremonies are still celebrated. By incorporating these traditional elements with newer ways of life, the Inuit are working to ensure that their culture will continue. As Inuk Fred Bigjim and Peace Corps volunteer James Ito-Adler once wrote, "We don't want a dead culture in a museum, we want a live culture." The Inuit have faced many challenges over their history, from their move across North America to their first encounters with Europeans and their efforts to gain a voice in politics. Through them all, the Inuit have adapted, accepting aspects of new cultures while holding fiercely to their own heritage.

IN THE FAR REACHES OF THE ARCTIC, ISOLATED INUIT VILLAGES STRIVE TO MAINTAIN THEIR CUSTOMS.

Among the Inuit, storytelling was a favorite way to pass the long, dark winters. Late into the night, Inuit elders shared stories that had been passed down for generations. Sometimes, they used a long ivory knife, known as a story knife, to draw pictures of their stories in the snow. Inuit stories dealt with survival, the Inuit way of life, the spirit world, and animals. This story, told by the Inuit of Canada, features the tricky wolverine and describes the creation of the northern lights.

Long ago, Wolverine walked alone through a village on a cloudy night. All the people were asleep. Seeing the moon in the sky, he used magic to jump up and shrink it. Then he stuffed it into a sack. He did the same with the sun. Then he ran to hide along the river.

When the villagers woke up the next day, it was still dark. The people were scared. They waited for hours, but neither the sun nor the moon came up. An orphan boy living near the village was great friends with the ravens. The ravens told him that Wolverine had stolen the sun and the moon. The boy told the villagers he would get the sun and the moon back.

The boy journeyed far along the river until he came to his aunt's house. He noticed she was wearing a new rabbit-fur coat. He realized only Wolverine could have caught enough rabbits to make the coat. His aunt confessed that Wolverine had given her the furs in return for a secret location far up-river to hide. She told the boy how to find the hiding spot.

After a long time, the boy came to the spot. He found Wolverine and tricked the animal into using his tail to sweep sunlight and moonlight out of his hut. Mixed in with the light was snow. The boy quickly formed snowballs and used magic to throw them into the sky. There, the snowballs burst into brilliant, moving curtains of light. Afterward, the boy threw more snowballs at Wolverine, who whimpered and did not fight back. Even though the fierce animal could hunt caribou and crack bones with his teeth, he was afraid of snowballs.

The boy grabbed the sun and the moon. He mixed their light in with more snowballs. Then he threw the snowballs into the sky, creating more northern lights. He kept throwing snowballs at Wolverine, too. Finally, the boy turned into a raven and went back to his village. He flew the sun and the moon up to the sky. From time to time, Wolverine tries to steal the sun and the moon again, but the boy simply chases him away with snowballs.

ALEUT
indigenous peoples of the Aleutian Islands and southwestern Alaska who are related to the Inuit

ANTHROPOLOGISTS
people who study the physical traits, cultures, and relationships of different peoples

ARCTIC
the northernmost part of the world, between the timberline (the farthest points north that trees grow) and the North Pole, including the Arctic Ocean

CACHES
hidden storage areas for food or other supplies

DIALECT
a form of a language that uses specific pronunciations, grammar, or vocabularies that differ from other forms of the language; speakers of different dialects of the same language can usually understand each other

ERIK THE RED
(c. mid-900s) Viking explorer who founded the first European settlement in Greenland

FIRST NATIONS
native peoples of Canada, excluding the Inuit and Métis

HARPOON
a fishing tool consisting of a spear attached to a rope

INDIGENOUS
native to a specific place

JAMES COOK
(1728–79) British naval officer who led three major expeditions in the Pacific, sailing as far north as the Bering Strait and as far south as Antarctica and claiming Australia for Britain

MARTIN FROBISHER
(c. 1535–94) English explorer who sailed the Canadian coastline in search of the Northwest Passage; while in Canada, he collected numerous rocks he thought contained gold but turned out to be worthless

NOMADIC
moving from place to place rather than living in a permanent home

SHAMAN
a spiritual leader often believed to have healing and other powers

SIBERIA
a region of northern Russia

SINEW
a tendon, or cord, that connects muscle to bone

SPAWNING
depositing eggs into water

TUNDRA
treeless, flat lands of the Arctic, where all but the top layer of soil remain frozen all year

VITUS BERING
(1681–1741) Danish explorer who sailed for Russia; he crossed the strait that would later bear his name, leading to the discovery that Russia and North America were not connected; Bering died after his ship was wrecked in Alaska

WEIRS
fences built in a river to trap fish

YUPIK
indigenous peoples of the southwestern Alaska coast who are related to the Inuit

Cassidy, James Jr., ed. *Through Indian Eyes: The Untold Story of Native American Peoples.* Pleasantville, N.Y.: Reader's Digest, 1995.

Damas, David, ed. *Arctic.* Vol. 5 of *Handbook of North American Indians.* Ed. William C. Sturtevant. Washington, D.C.: Smithsonian, 1984.

Harper, Kenn. *In Those Days: Collected Writings on Arctic History. Book 1: Inuit Lives.* Toronto: Inhabit Media, 2013.

Josephy, Alvin M., Jr. *500 Nations: An Illustrated History of North American Indians.* New York: Knopf, 1994.

Norman, Howard. *The Girl Who Dreamed Only Geese, and Other Tales of the Far North.* San Diego: Gulliver Books, 1997.

Time-Life Editors. *People of the Ice and Snow.* Alexandria, Va.: Time-Life Books, 1994.

Waldman, Carl. *Atlas of the North American Indian.* 3rd ed. New York: Checkmark Books, 2009.

Wright, Shelley. *Our Ice is Vanishing: A History of the Inuit, Newcomers, and Climate Change.* Montreal, Quebec: McGill-Queen's University, 2014.

⊰⇒ READ MORE ⇐⊱

Dwyer, Helen, ed. *Peoples of the Southwest, West, and North.* Redding, Conn.: Brown Bear Books, 2009.

Sharp, Anne Wallace. *The Inuit.* San Diego: Lucent Books, 2002.

⊰⇒ WEBSITES ⇐⊱

INUIT CULTURAL ONLINE RESOURCE
http://icor.ottawainuitchildrens.com/
Check out information and photos about Inuit history, culture, and modern life.

INUVIALUIT REGIONAL CORPORATION
http://www.irc.inuvialuit.com/culture
Learn more about Inuit culture, including games, music, and clothing.